Nature's Children

ANTEATERS

Lorien Kite

GROLIER
EDUCATIONAL

FACTS IN BRIEF

Classification of Anteaters

Class: *Mammalia* (mammals)
Order: *Edentata*
Family: *Myrmecophagidae* (hairy anteaters)
Genus: *Myrmecophaga*
Species: *Myrmecophaga tridactyla* (giant anteater)

World distribution.   South and Central America.

Habitat.   Savannas, forests, and swamplands.

Distinctive physical characteristics.   Narrow, tubelike snout; extremely long, wormlike tongue; large, curved claws; mainly gray-brown in color; large, bulky tail; coarse coat of hair, very long on the back and tail.

Habits.   Solitary and territorial. Defends itself ferociously when attacked. Active mainly during the day. Young are born singly and carried on their mothers' backs. Generally silent, communicates by scent marking. Strong swimmer.

Diet.   Ants and termites.

CIP information available from the Library of Congress or the publisher

This library reinforced edition is available exclusively from:

GROLIER
EDUCATIONAL

Sherman Turnpike, Danbury, Connecticut 06816

Editor: James Kinchen Designer: Tim Brown
Printed and Bound in U.S.A.   Set ISBN 0-7172-9351-3

Contents

Imagine yourself alone on a South American savanna. An endless carpet of swaying grass, sparsely scattered with thorn bushes and small trees, stretches to the horizon.

In the distance you see a dark shape moving slowly through the tall grasses. Its body and enormous tail are covered with coarse gray-brown hair. Black diagonal stripes run up each side of its back. Holding its narrow, tubelike snout close to the ground, it stops once every few steps to tap the earth with a long, curved claw.

This is the giant anteater, searching for insects in the sun-baked earth. It may look strange to you—but this shy, solitary creature is perfectly designed for the life it leads. Read on to learn all about this fascinating animal.

Wandering across the savanna, the shy and solitary giant anteater is rarely seen by people.

Anteater Territory

In this book you will learn about the hairy anteaters of South and Central America. Of the four types, or species, in this family of animals, the largest is the giant anteater. From the tip of its snout to the end of its tail, this creature is longer than a fully grown man lying on his back.

Giant anteaters live in a range of habitats, including swamplands, rain forests, and dry woodlands. Their favorite places, however, are the vast, open savannas that lie both north and south of the great Amazon rain forest.

Found in tropical parts of the world, savannas are hot, grassy plains with few trees. For a few months each year it rains heavily, but for the rest of the time it is very dry. Savannas are very rich in wildlife, and many have been made into large nature reserves.

During the brief rainy season the savannas of South America often become flooded.

Undercover Insects

When they are not sleeping, giant anteaters spend almost all of their time searching for food. They live on ants and termites—and need to eat at least 30,000 of them every day! Fortunately for the anteaters, these tiny insects live together in huge, well-organized groups. Despite their small size, enough can be caught at one time to make up a decent meal.

Termites live in large mounds that they build by chewing up earth and mixing it with their own saliva to make a kind of liquid cement. Termite mounds can stand 12 feet (four meters) tall and may contain many millions of insects.

Giant anteaters prefer to eat types of ants that build their nests underground. Although they are less obvious than termite mounds, underground ant nests can be even bigger, covering areas the size of football fields.

Baked by the sun, the earth walls of a termite mound become as hard as rock, protecting the insects inside.

Anteater Senses

Ants and termites rarely leave their nests. Protected by fierce guards, the queen remains deep inside the nest throughout her life, laying eggs that will hatch into new members of the colony. Her workers occasionally venture out to collect food, but even they spend most of their time hidden away, traveling through a vast network of covered feeding trails.

Giant anteaters hardly seem equipped to track down these cautious insects. Their hearing is poor, and their vision is even worse. You would probably be able to creep up to within 30 feet (10 meters) of one before it noticed you were there.

What anteaters do have, however, is an extremely powerful sense of smell. By holding their sensitive snouts close to the ground, giant anteaters are able to sniff out insect colonies with pinpoint accuracy.

A giant anteater concentrates on sniffing out some ants.

A giant anteater walks on its knuckles, keeping its long claws tucked away to stop them from being worn down by the hard ground.

Tools of the Trade

It is not easy to break through the sun-baked earth of the savanna, and even harder to get into a termite mound. Without a sharp spade or a pickaxe you would find it impossible.

The giant anteater's four-to-six inch (10-to-15 centimeter) front claws enable it to break into ant nests and termite mounds with ease. To keep them razor-sharp, it scratches at trees whenever it gets the chance.

One of the claws on a giant anteater's front foot is much bigger than the others. Why do you think this is so? If you need a clue, think how easy it is to push a thumbtack into a wall. This task is simple because all of your strength is being concentrated on one tiny point. The giant anteater's long claw works in the same way, allowing it to break through the hardest of barriers.

Surprise Attack!

Once a giant anteater has located its meal, it carefully makes a few holes in the earth with its long claw. Then, after widening the hole with a few circular movements of the snout, it flicks its tongue deep into the nest, throwing the insects into confusion.

A giant anteater's tongue is truly amazing. Longer than your arm, it can thrust about 22 inches (55 centimeters) into a nest, darting in and out of the anteater's mouth at a rate of 160 strokes per minute. On each return journey tiny inward-pointing spikes on the tongue sweep the insects out of their nests and into the anteater's stomach.

An anteater covers its tongue in thick, sticky saliva. This turns the tongue into a natural flypaper, ideal for collecting small insects.

Fast Food

Have you ever been so hungry that you gulped down your food without chewing it properly? You probably got stomach pains later on and regretted having eaten so quickly.

Giant anteaters, on the other hand, never chew their food—they have no teeth to chew with! To make up for this, they have extremely muscular stomachs that can grind up food before they digest it. The earth and gravel that anteaters swallow by accident also helps to crush up the insects in their stomachs.

One advantage of eating in this way is that it is very fast. Giant anteaters need to eat as quickly as possible, for each of their meals is a race against time. Why do they have to eat fast? It may surprise you, but the anteater's prey are not as helpless as their small size might suggest.

After breaking into a rotting log, a giant anteater feeds on the ants that have made their nest inside.

Mighty Ants

Just like humans, many ant and termite species have armies that rush to defend their homes as soon as they realize that they have been attacked. Like human soldiers, they are specially armed for their role. They have large pincers, or mandibles, which they use to bite intruders. Another similarity between ant and human soldiers is that, when all else fails, both are prepared to sacrifice their lives in a desperate attempt to ward off the enemy. Bravely, they launch themselves at the anteater, swarming up its nose and biting hard on its tongue.

By the time the soldiers arrive on the scene, hundreds of insects will have already perished. Once the biting starts, however, the anteater becomes so irritated that it moves on, leaving the insects to count their losses and rebuild.

A queen termite surrounded by her guards and workers. The guards are slightly bigger than the workers and have large pincers on their heads.

Poison!

As if biting weren't bad enough on its own, many ant species have poisons in their bodies and can inject venom with their pincers. If an anteater were to dine on only one type of ant, it might get sick. To cope with this, anteaters range far and wide when they hunt. Because there are thousands of species of ants, moving on frequently allows the anteater to make sure that it eats many different types in the course of a day. By feeding in this way, many different poisons can be absorbed in small, harmless quantities.

Not all ants bite or poison their attackers. Some just run away. In the savanna their nests are often so big that they can eventually outdistance the giant anteater's searching tongue. So why don't giant anteaters simply dig farther in to root out the fleeing insects? Turn the page to find out.

An ant soldier ready to attack.
Anteaters try to avoid the most
poisonous species of ants.

Creatures of Habit

Because anteaters are territorial animals, they are lucky that the insects they live on are so hard to catch. Day after day, year after year, they walk the same paths, often going back to trusted spots where they know they can get a good meal. If an anteater were to wipe out all the ants in its territory, it would have to move somewhere else.

If you were to follow an anteater and inspect the places where it has fed, you would hardly notice any damage. Anteaters are not pointlessly destructive. In fact, they take care not to damage nests beyond the point of repair. In a way, anteaters are like farmers, carefully managing their resources so that they last a lifetime and beyond. Humans would do well to take note!

Worker and guard termites quickly move in to repair the damage to their nests.

Get Off My Land!

An anteater patrols a territory of up to nine square miles (23 square kilometers). Although their territories usually overlap slightly at the edges, meetings between these solitary creatures are extremely rare. If two meet up on shared land, they usually just ignore one another and wander off in opposite directions.

When a stranger strays too far into its territory, however, an anteater will circle the intruder menacingly. If it doesn't clear off immediately, the anteater whose territory it is will start pushing or even slashing at the unwelcome guest with its claws. Such fights can occasionally lead to serious injuries.

Humans are the greatest threat to the giant anteater. The destruction of their savannas has forced them to live in an increasingly small area, where fighting and starvation have reduced their numbers to dangerous levels.

On its own patch an anteater definitely prefers to be left alone.

Tooth versus Claw

Giant anteaters have few natural predators. Their huge tails and bushy coats make them look even bigger than they are, so they are only rarely attacked by the pumas and jaguars that share their habitat. Giant anteaters are careful, too, and gallop off at the slightest hint of trouble. The big cats, however, are faster runners, and sometimes an anteater will just have to stand and fight.

Although it only ever fights in self-defense, the giant anteater is a formidable opponent. Using its tail to help it to balance, a cornered anteater will rear up on its hind legs and draw back its muscular forearms. Then, falling forward, it will fling its arms around the enemy, stabbing it with its huge claws.

Big cats do not usually dare to attack giant anteaters. They could easily end up severely injured—or at worst, dead.

Even jaguars, the largest cats in South America, only attack giant anteaters when desperate for food.

Fire and Water

Each year, when the rains come, many of the rivers that flow through the great plains of northern Brazil and Venezuela burst their banks, causing huge floods. Luckily giant anteaters are strong swimmers. Even in the dry season they often cross large rivers in the course of their daily wanderings.

With much of the savanna underwater, however, it becomes harder for anteaters to find their favorite types of ant. They are forced to eat more termites, which, safe in their mounds, are able to survive the floods.

Even so, giant anteaters are probably glad when the rains come. By the end of the long dry season the land is so parched that fires can start easily, spreading quickly through the savanna. With their coats of long, coarse hair, giant anteaters catch fire easily. They are often found burned to a crisp after these fires.

Fire spreads quickly through the dry grass of the savanna. Anteaters must be alert to stay out of trouble.

Wherever I Lay My Tail

Giant anteaters sleep for about 14 hours each day. They often take short naps after a meal to sleep off the effects of any poisons in their food, and in isolated, safe areas they also like to sleep throughout the night. Giant anteaters that live near towns or villages, however, often move only under the cover of darkness, sleeping through the daylight hours to avoid any contact with people.

Giant anteaters are not that choosy about where they sleep. Sometimes they shelter in abandoned burrows or hollow logs, but usually they just find a sheltered ditch and bed down under the stars. For protection from the sun, rain, or cold, they simply tuck their long snouts between their forelegs and cover their bodies with their huge tails. If you were to pass a sleeping anteater, you would probably mistake it for a bush!

With its nose between its paws, a giant anteater rests in the sunshine.

Two giant anteaters play together in a zoo.

Lean on Me

In most areas the giant anteater mating season runs from March to May, although matings can occur throughout the year. You would be wrong if you thought that these unsociable creatures found it hard to find mates. When the time is right, a female giant anteater gives off an extremely strong scent. Sooner or later a nearby male picks up this scent and tracks the female down. To show his interest, he touches her gently with his paw and lays his head on her back. The two anteaters then spend the rest of the day playfighting and getting to know one another.

After mating, the two go their separate ways, never to meet again. Six months later a single baby is born.

Piggyback Rider

As soon as a giant anteater is born, it climbs up onto its mother's back and buries its head in her coat. This is where it will spend most of the next six months.

It is only when you see a giant anteater with her baby that you understand the purpose of her black diagonal stripes. While in piggyback position, the baby's stripe finishes off its mother's. With its tiny head buried in her coat, it blends in perfectly, and the two look like one animal. So what passing pumas and jaguars see is not a small and vulnerable meal, but one particularly large anteater—not to be interfered with!

The baby anteater drinks its mother's milk for several months, but it is already interested in ants. It scampers up close when mom breaks into a nest and slurps up any ants that wander its way.

Hidden in its mother's furry coat, a baby giant anteater is safe from predators.

Play with Me, Mom!

A young anteater is a playful creature. Unfortunately, it has no one to play with apart from its mom! It loves dancing around her and challenging her with mock attacks. Tolerant and protective, mom usually responds by laying her head on the youngster's back—her way of saying "Calm down!"

At about six months old giant anteaters begin to make short, careful trips away from their mothers to explore their surroundings. At the first sign of trouble, however, they scamper back onto the safety of their mothers' backs. Even after nine months, when they are almost as big as their mothers, they still try to jump on. At this point, however, mom does her best to dodge her big baby. Weighing in at 65 pounds (30 kilograms), the young anteater is much too heavy for her to carry around.

Life Cycle

At about one year old a giant anteater is fully grown, although it will need another six months or so to attain its full weight of about 120 pounds (55 kilograms). Its mother has taught it how to survive on its own, but there are not enough ants in her territory to support them both. Sadly, it leaves its mother to find its own territory. It may have to travel a long way before finding the perfect spot, and it will almost certainly never see her again.

Throughout its life the giant anteater will face danger from big cats, other anteaters, fires, floods, and most of all, humans. After about three or four years it will be able to have children of its own. If it is very lucky, it will wander the plains for its full life span of about 25 years—by which time it will have eaten well over 200 million ants!

At Home in the Trees

Tropical rain forests crawl with insects. Here, ants and termites build their nests high up in the trees, way out of the giant anteater's reach. Getting at these insects is no problem for the other members of the hairy anteater family. Both the tamandua and the silky anteater are perfectly at home in the trees.

A tamandua is about the size of a cat. Unlike the giant anteater, the tamandua can use its tail to grasp hold of branches when it climbs. This gives it extra security in the trees.

As well as a grasping tail, the squirrel-sized silky anteater has large pads on its forepaws and feet, which form natural grooves for thin branches. The silky anteater's grip is so strong that even when it loses its balance it can still hold on, hanging upside down.

A tamandua grips a tree trunk with its strong tail, helping it to climb down safely.

Forest Stinker

In proportion to their bodies, tamanduas have shorter snouts than giant anteaters, and their ears and eyes are larger. Their coloring varies from blond to dark brown. Tamanduas from central and southern parts of South America also have black "vests" on their coats.

Tamanduas look clumsy on land and cannot gallop. Even so, there are many living in savannas and croplands. They are by far the most common kind of anteater.

To mark their territories, tamanduas produce a foul-smelling liquid that lingers on everything they touch. The Guarani tribe of the Amazon rain forest hate it so much that their name for the tamandua is *caguaré*, which means "forest stinker."

Like giant anteaters, tamanduas rear up on their back legs and show their claws when threatened.

Tightrope Walker

The silky anteater gets its name from the silvery or golden yellow color of its smooth coat. It is completely nocturnal and never comes down to the ground.

Because of their small size silky anteaters are particularly vulnerable to enemies such as snakes and prowling wildcats, and they spend most of their time on thin branches where these animals cannot reach. Even there they are not completely safe. They may be carried off by swooping eagles, owls, and hawks.

Perhaps because of this danger from above, silky anteaters spend most of their time in the kapok, or silk-cotton tree. This tree is covered with soft, silvery seed pods. Side by side a silky anteater and a seed pod look almost identical, especially at night, so the anteater is not spotted by passing predators.

The common but rarely seen silky anteater feeds on beetles and fruits in addition to ants and termites.

Distant Cousins?

There are animals in Africa, Asia, and Australia that, at first glance, look curiously similar to the South American hairy anteaters. Aardvarks, pangolins, and spiny anteaters all have long snouts, wormlike tongues, and powerful claws, and they also feed on insects.

Scientists used to think that all these animals were related to one another. They classed them as *edentates*, which means "animals without teeth." Had they looked a little more closely, they might have realized that aardvarks, pangolins, and spiny anteaters all have small, barely noticeable teeth. Hairy anteaters are the only members of the group with none at all.

We now know that none of these animals are closely related. They only look similar because they all specialize in eating insects. Because of this confusion hairy anteaters are also called "true" anteaters.

Words to Know

Amazon rain forest The largest rain forest in the world, covering most of central and northern Brazil.

Big cat One of a group of large hunting cats that includes lions, tigers, and jaguars.

Colony A group of animals that live together.

Habitat The area in which an animal naturally lives.

Insect One of a large family of creatures with six legs and three body sections. Bees, ants, and flies are all insects.

Nocturnal Active only at night.

Predator An animal that hunts other animals for food.

Prey An animal that is hunted and eaten by other animals.

Queen The ruler of a colony of insects. The queen lays eggs that hatch into new workers and guards for the colony.

Rain forest A dense tropical forest in an area of high rainfall. Rain forests are extremely rich in plant and animal life.

Termites Insects that live in large colonies either in trees or in mounds of hard earth. Termites are very common in tropical regions. They feed mainly on decaying leaves and wood.

Territory Area where an animal hunts or breeds, which it defends against other animals.

Venom A harmful chemical injected through a bite or sting.

INDEX

Cover Photo: Haroldo Palo Jr. / NHPA
Photo Credits: Tom Brakefield / Corbis, pages 4, 15, 16, 27; Joel Creed; Ecoscene / Corbis, pages 7, 8; Joe McDonald / Corbis, pages 11, 31; Daniel Heuclin / NHPA, page 12; Haroldo Palo Jr. / NHPA, pages 19, 35, 38; Darren Maybury; Eye Ubiquitous / Corbis, page 20; Peter Johnson / © Corbis, page 23; Jany Sauvanet / NHPA, pages 24, 40, 43, 44; Richard Hamilton Smith / Corbis, page 28; George Lepp / Corbis, page 32.